Never For Difference Yo

Teachers plant the seeds of knowledge
that last a lifetime.

Owl always love teaching.

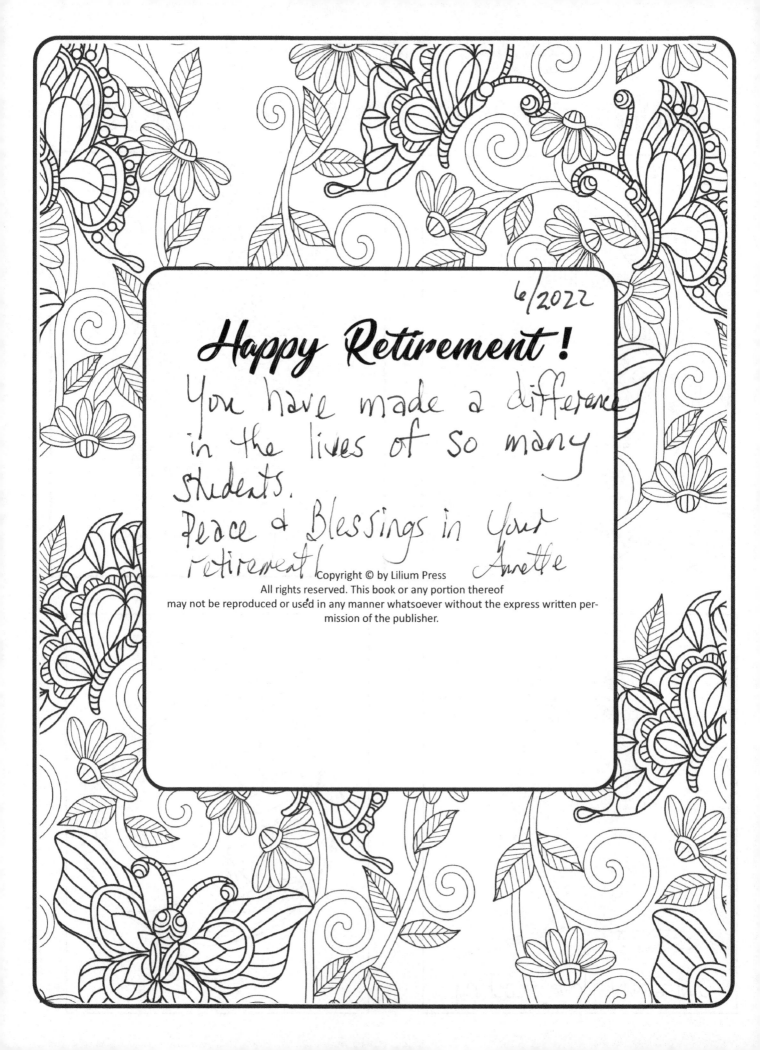

Happy Retirement!

You have made a difference in the lives of so many students.

Peace & Blessings in Your retirement!

Annette

6/2022

This book belongs to:

Jeanne Cashin

In case no one told you today; you are a great teacher!

Only the brave teach.

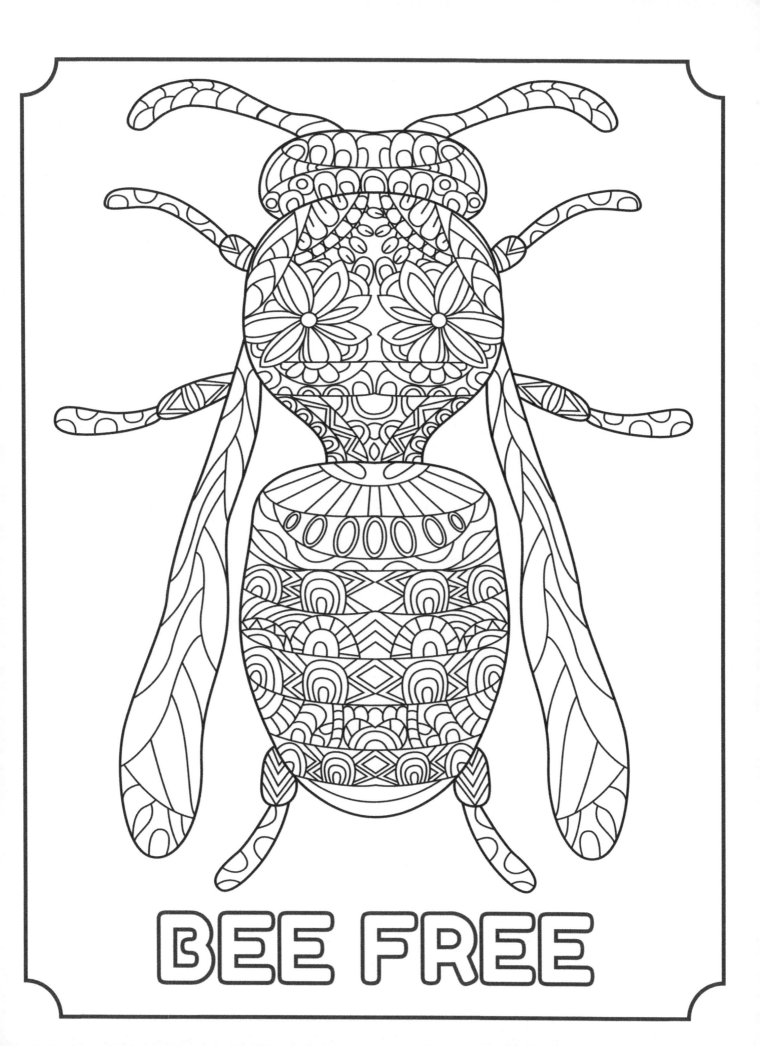

BEE FREE

Teaching is the greatest act of optimism.

Teachers plant the seeds of knowledge that last a lifetime.

Teachers who love teaching teach children to love learning.

You will be missed!

Retirement

is magical

Owl always love teaching.

A teacher takes a hand, opens a mind and touches a heart.

Teaching is the only job where you steal things from home and bring them to work.

You can't retire from being awesome!

To teach is to touch a life forever.